A Simple Guide To The World Of Aesthetics For Pharmacists

This book is your step by step route to aesthetic success

By Amar Suchde

A Simple Guide To The World Of Aesthetics For Pharmacists
Published in 2017 by Urban Media Publishing Ltd
Copyright © 2020 by Amar Suchde
Editors: Sachin Patel
Amar can be reached at Amar@pharm-aesthetics.uk

Amar Suchde has asserted his moral rights to be identified as the author of this work in accordance with the Copyright, Designs and Patents Act 1988. All rights reserved. Apart from any permitted use under UK copyright law no part of this publication may be reproduced, stored in a retrieval system or transmitted in any form or by any means, electronic, mechanical, photocopying, recording or otherwise, without the prior written permission of the publishers and copyright holders.

First published 2017

ISBN 978-1720452799

Urban Media Publishing Ltd,
1-5 Shambles,
York YO1 7LZ.
Web: urbanmediapublishing.co.uk

DEDICATION

This book is dedicated to:

My grandad-for his belief and faith in me

My mum Nita- you are the best. Thank you for everything

My dad Manish-I'm grateful that you pushed me.

My uncle Ronak - for giving me a stepping stone

Kwame - to my older brother, thank you for being there and helping me understand things a lot better. It will always be appreciated!

Shilpa & Mitesh- For helping me when I doubted myself

To all my friends who supported me and were there during my early growing stages - you are the best.

To Sachin Patel for your help with this book. It doesn't go unnoticed.

Introduction

One reason for writing this book is that so many people have approached me to ask how I managed to get into aesthetics and then build a thriving business with a chain of clinics in a relatively short time. This question is often followed by a request for me to spend time with someone to explain more about how I managed to make the leap from pharmacy into aesthetics.

I am happy to help most people because I have had to work very hard to get into the position I find myself today. I will explain in detail within this book how I managed to progress my business but the key turning point for me was to find a mentor because I am a big believer in mentoring and I became the protégé of one of the best aesthetic practitioners in the UK who deals with famous people and celebrities.

Thanks to my mentor, I learned a lot very quickly which helped me to toughen up and take a more pragmatic viewpoint of what I wanted to do and where I wanted to be with my business. I am not saying that the journey will be easy for other pharmacists who want to follow these footsteps; I had dark days and great days from the beginning, but it is possible for pharmacists with similar experiences to develop a lucrative and thriving aesthetics business.

Most of my fellow pharmacists who approach me have the same passion as I do for the treatment of skin and the well-being of their patients. Perhaps the hardest part of the building-up of an aesthetics business is to develop and grow a reputation for excellence which will suit the mindset of many pharmacists.

Unfortunately, because I was so busy in running my clinics and developing my business, I did not have the time to help many of those asking for advice. I did help whenever possible and found the experience rewarding as well as informative. Everyone who came to me has had a different outlook on how they wanted to develop their business and I knew from the beginning of setting out on my journey that I wanted to write a book about my experiences and to help others follow in my footsteps.

I have no doubts that everyone's journey to business success could make for an informative book for someone else to follow in their path. Just recently I attended an aesthetics event and it became apparent that there is a handful of people out there who share the same passion as I do for helping people with skin problems. For many, aesthetics is a career path they would love to go down and hopefully someone reading this book will benefit hugely from my experience of what has been a tough journey. There is no doubt too that it would have been a lot tougher without my finding an excellent mentor in the shape of Dr Vincent Wong.

I will explain the effort that I went to in trying to get into the industry and then the effort I made in making contact with Dr Wong. Since meeting with Dr Wong I have never looked back but I always bear in mind his initial advice which was that his first year in business was the toughest year of his life.

Dr Wong left a permanent job as a doctor in the NHS to focus on a career in an incredibly competitive industry and since setting out he has achieved a lot of success but this has only come after hard work and dedication.

I also left behind a well-paid permanent job as a pharmacist and I remember saying to Dr Wong that I was fortunate to be part of his journey and experience and that I would benefit from that and in turn would help someone else benefit too.

It is important to remember that time is valuable and I proposed that Dr Wong and I began a business together to work alongside each other to help people make a success of a business within aesthetics.

There is no doubt that the industry is expanding at a rapid rate and looking to do so for many years yet, so there is room and opportunity for all of us. This is also a good time because legislation governing who can and cannot carry out aesthetic treatments is being tightened continually.

I sincerely believe that pharmacists have the training, experience and the qualifications to make a success of delivering aesthetic treatments to their patients and help promote the high standards and qualities that we all should be working towards.

This book is aimed at a variety of healthcare professionals that are looking at getting into aesthetics, though it will appeal to pharmacists wanting to enjoy a rewarding business opportunity and will provide the guidance and information they are looking for to create a successful aesthetic business. Furthermore, it is also about the journey and progress I have made to get where I am today and, make no mistake, the journey will continue to ever greater success. For anyone in pharmacy who would like to make this step then this book will provide the necessary advice and guidance to a rewarding and thoroughly enjoyable new career.

Amar Suchde
London

Chapter 1

My experience/ journey

I am a registered pharmacist and aesthetic practitioner with a keen interest in improving the health and well-being of my patients. The internal and external health benefits that a drug or a medical treatment can exhibit on the human body have always been of great interest to me.

A business-minded upbringing, together with a Master's degree in pharmacy provided a platform for me to create a self-sustaining business that would also allow me to fulfil my desire to help my patients.

So, what sparked this interest you may ask? Well, I spent a large proportion of my childhood in Great Ormond Street Hospital due to health issues; namely eczema and asthma. As a result, I was subject to regular regimens of oral and topical medication. This early exposure to such medical treatments, the topical form in particular, sprung my initial interest in aesthetics.

The concept of a topical formulation improving the quality of my skin and, in turn, my self-esteem amazed me. During my years at university studying pharmacy, eczema and asthma are the two subject areas that became a core focus for me. In addition, whenever I was given a project choice, I would always choose something that was skin-related.

Eventually, I qualified as a pharmacist and I went to work in the community for a variety of different pharmacies. I left this area of work because I was so despondent working for an organisation that was purely target driven; I wanted to help people but I felt at the time as though I was not actually helping people. There is no doubt that I learned a lot, it proved to be a great training ground but ultimately, I found the world of targets and ticking boxes thoroughly unsatisfactory and had to move on to other things.

As my career as a pharmacist progressed, I was still obsessed about skin and how to improve it; this interest eventually led me to the world of aesthetics. To my mind, the universe works in a special way and everything I have done previously fell into place when I came across the potential for helping people to enhance the appearance of their skin via aesthetics. In many ways, looking back it was a natural path into the industry and I have had excellent preparation in pursuing this as my vocation.

I have always believed strongly in the purpose of having a mentor. In June of 2014, I met Dr Vincent Wong - one of the youngest, up-and-coming talents in aesthetics who agreed to become my mentor and he is still a good friend today. He is a very busy man who had given me a short window of time and so agreed to meet with me in a coffee shop in Marylebone. Whilst under the realisation and pressure of this very rare opportunity, I managed to keep my composure and be my usual charismatic self, which highlighted to Dr Wong the benefits that would arise for both of us from him mentoring me.

Essentially, I believe I put across my passion about learning more about aesthetics, about skin and about helping people feel better about themselves in their own skin.

Let it be noted at this stage however, finding a mentor as well established, skilled and generous in sharing one's knowledge as Dr Wong is like finding a needle in a haystack.

Getting into aesthetics can be a difficult and daunting task; I mean I literally knocked on a thousand doors before I even met the inspirational man who was to become my aesthetics mentor.

It is not just about developing a career or business; a mentor can help on other levels too. One reason I recommend a mentor is that unless you have the relevant contacts and experience it is quite difficult to progress within many industries and having the opportunity to use someone else's experiences can prove beneficial for both people.

Moving into aesthetics means creating a business that is both rewarding and fulfilling at the same time. One of the big attractions for me is that aesthetics in the UK is a relatively untapped market and I was intrigued and inspired to be one of the relatively few pharmacists to make the crossover into the industry and make a success of it. For those who wonder whether I have made the right decision, bear in mind that the aesthetics industry in the UK is set to treble in size over the coming years to be worth more than £3 billion.

In the year I started in aesthetics there was the introduction to clamp down on the practices already in place because too many people were exploiting the needs of patients without having the necessary skills or experience. Thankfully, the industry is making steps towards tightening regulations so that patients are protected more from people who should not be delivering aesthetic treatments. I accept completely that legislation is necessary to prevent unqualified and ill-trained people from giving aesthetic treatments and there were concerns then that just about anyone could set up a business after minimal training. The mentorship provided to me by Dr Wong has paved a path for me in aesthetics via thorough clinical training in injectables, the relevant business skills required to succeed and expert guidance in becoming an ethical practitioner.

Since starting out as an aesthetic practitioner, there have indeed been days where I have found myself sat in a room waiting for things to happen and it has taken 18 months to build a chain of six clinics including a clinic in Harley Street and in Sloane Square. The reason I mention this is because there will be days when you will question whether you have made the right decision but, eventually, the clinic will become more successful with a growing client base and, as a result, will begin to flourish as a self-sustaining business and source of income.

After reading this book, If you are interested in following Mr Suchde's exact steps- then join his elite mentorship package where you will be mentored by him and various leading doctors in the industry, including the famous Dr V Wong. Just email us at Amar@pharm-aesthetics.uk.

You will never look back and as a pharmacist it will be best move you ever make!

A Simple Guide To The World Of Aesthetics For Pharmacists

Chapter 2

How pharmacists can be successful aesthetic practitioners

One of the reasons I believe that pharmacists make excellent aesthetic practitioners is that they regularly carry out consultations with their patients and learn to ask the correct questions to find out what they need to know. There is no doubt that my own training and pharmacy experiences have helped me deal with my patients in my clinics.

It also helps that I am an outgoing person, friendly and a very effective communicator and relationship builder, a skillset largely developed during my pharmacy career. This, in combination with the high quality results of my treatments, means that most of my clients come to me through word-of-mouth. This has proven to be an invaluable advertising tool since most of it is due to my hard-earned reputation.

It should also be appreciated that while the aesthetics industry in the UK is growing rapidly and that there are a lot of medical professionals with various backgrounds and specialties helping to meet the demand, there is only a limited supply of potential clients. Furthermore, clients wanting aesthetic treatments are not wanting to have cosmetic procedures - the two offerings are worlds apart. It is important to appreciate early on also that at no point will an aesthetic practitioner put a client under the knife to carry out the treatment; this is the work of experienced professionals who need to carry out a thorough consultation beforehand.

So, while it may appear that a client wanting non-surgical cosmetic treatments, may be doing so because they cannot afford or want a surgical cosmetic treatment, it does not mean that their choice should be limited. Aesthetic practitioners need to be as professional as their cosmetic counterparts and offer a high level of customer service - a service that a pharmacist will be familiar with providing. Failure to deliver or meet a client's expectations will see them moving to another practitioner in a bid to find someone who can meet his or her needs. It will become apparent that clients will not hesitate to move to a different practitioner if they are not satisfied and, if your practice is not seeing high levels of client retention, then you must analyse the quality of your work and customer service.

I should also make clear that I refer to those who come to me as a client and not as patients because there is a distinction between the two. Throughout this book I will always refer to clients because we are offering help and advice, which they do not have to accept – and they do not have to use our expertise. A patient will often demure to the physician's advice and follow what they are advised. The other issue to bear in mind is that this is not a traditional pharmacist/patient relationship and that the aesthetics practitioner must work harder to win their client's trust and to retain their business.

It's also crucial that training is at the forefront of all practitioners' work and they should undergo regular training sessions to find out the latest products that are available on the market – once again, a pre-existing aspect of a pharmacist's role. On top of this, the practitioner will also need business training because we need to make our practice a success and to deliver the quality of life we are expecting. It's our level of training and professionalism that will help attract clients because we will be competing in the sector where there are qualified doctors and nurses, as well as dentists, trying to attract clients to their practice.

For those setting out on the path to creating an aesthetics practice, it will soon become apparent that pricing is a crucial element of attracting and retaining clients. However, it would be foolhardy to believe that a practice will become a success by simply offering treatments at a lower price than any other rival. There are a number of reasons why new practitioners should not engage in a price war with competitors because it will mean having to carry out more treatments for more clients so it means working longer in the clinic for a diminishing return. This will benefit no one and by not generating sufficient profit the practitioner will not create a business to support them but also fail to generate the income for future success. It is also important to realise that clients will differentiate between practitioners on the level of service because of the price they charge; charge a low price and many clients will avoid your offering because they will worry about the quality they will receive.

Essentially, the secret for a successful aesthetics practice is to focus solely on delivering the very best results for clients at the price they are happy to pay. By focusing on this client relationship, the practitioner will create a business where client retention and an expanding client base will bring financial and personal success. This client relationship happens to us all; for instance, I go to one barber to cut my hair and I have done for several years because I am happy with the service and the price I pay and I get on very well with him. It is this emotional bonding with my barber that ensures I will always be a returning customer and for me to switch barbers means I will need several very good reasons for doing so. As pharmacists, this may not yet be as clear-cut, however we will look more closely at this aspect in this book because it is part of promotion and this relationship marketing is a vital element within that.

Chapter 3

Training

As anyone with a medical background, and that includes pharmacists like myself, will know that training and continual personal/professional development is a lifelong process – knowledge is power. Therefore, as an aesthetic practitioner, ongoing training and personal/professional development will be crucial to the success of your business enterprise and it is important to become an expert in the treatments being delivered.

At the basic level of practice, the practitioner must appreciate that there is an established principle as to how we define beauty. A fresh complexion and youthfulness is often regarded as an indication of beauty that has evolved in recent years to include having a beautiful smile with healthy gums and teeth.

Many people also consider high cheekbones and beautiful lips, as well as large ascending eyes to complete facial symmetry; this has led to the development of the 'golden ratio'. One of the most popular questions that arises within aesthetics is, 'What is beauty?' The golden ratio offers the dimensions that will help provide the answer, particularly when treating clients.

Part of the training the aesthetic practitioner will undertake is to have an ability to carry out a facial assessment to an expert level. As the industry grows and competition increases along with it there is pressure to attract new clients and this appreciation of beauty will be crucial.

Sadly, facial balance and proportionality is not always appreciated. One reason why an appreciation of the golden ratio is proving to be increasingly important is that the practitioner needs to be aware that whatever treatment they carry out may have an impact on the overall look of the client. That is why many people say that it is much like building a house - the foundations must be correct and the structure takes place around it.

An in-depth understanding of the ageing process is a key aspect of a practitioner's training. The process ultimately compromises a person's facial dimensions and the facial structure may lead to a less attractive appearance. The practitioner will need a knowledge base of the effects of ageing on the external and internal features. This will lead to a consistent level of high quality treatment results and thus exceed the expectations of the client.

The aesthetics industry has developed very quickly; a new practitioner would have done well financially even 10 years ago by simply offering anti-wrinkle treatments. A rapid growth in competition has diminished what was once an exclusive trade, which would have been sought only from specific high-end clinics, such as those found on Harley Street, and has now begun to find its way on to the high streets. Therefore, the quality of a practitioner's training and expertise will be a more significant and differentiating factor than ever before between one practice and the next.

Clients wanting aesthetics treatments are also more knowledgeable and more demanding with their needs so a practitioner should be well trained and, this could be crucial, well informed about the latest developments and treatments. Clients will inevitably ask about them so the practitioner must offer an opinion about the request or offer the treatment itself. Product manufacturers regularly hold training events that can be very interesting and rewarding, they are also a great opportunity for networking. Indeed, some of the conferences that are organised are enjoyable and many are held in nice locations so attendees can have a holiday as well.

I would point out that if funds are short then any money available should be spent on specific training, that a training plan is put into place and then acted upon. There is no doubt that by continual development a practitioner will achieve their planned business success. One aspect of training that is often overlooked is the 'soft' people skills that are required to help attract and retain clients. I believe communication is a key part of the process in building a practice and it is something that can be learnt and polished. Communicating effectively with clients, along with colleagues, means there will not be any misunderstandings about a treatment and a client will appreciate what the result will be.

Many clients are influenced by what they read and believe that a treatment will be a huge success when that may not be the case since our faces are different. This is why communication is crucial during the consultation because it will identify what a client really needs and then help deliver a realistic appreciation of what the final result will be. If your practice is to offer a wide range of treatments, then learning how to communicate their effectiveness will help to improve sales in what is an increasingly competitive market. Creating a real bond with the client in that initial meeting is important and will mean they will return again and again as well as recommending you and your practice to their friends and family.

Should you undertake communication training, you will soon learn there are three different styles - passive, assertive and aggressive. Each one suits a different type of person but appreciating which style you use is the secret to effective communication. Practitioners should always be diplomatic since the client is attending a consultation because they may have issues with their appearance and want you to help resolve them. These issues need to be discussed in a delicate manner without causing offence; it is a tricky situation as you will probably have to ask searching questions to find out what the client needs and wants are to deliver the very best treatments to make them happy.

We should also view communication as a sales skill. Let's be honest, we want our practice to be as successful as possible, which means that during the client's initial consultation we need to use our communication skills to 'close the deal'. I acknowledge that while we as aesthetic practitioners do a lot of great work we are essentially selling our skills and our expertise. Do not shy away from the fact that we need to sell to a client and if we recognise the possibility of selling them another treatment as well, then we should do so if it benefits the client. Failure to close a sale means having to work harder to find new clients and sell them a treatment; this is a skill and it needs to be worked upon.

In the next chapter I discuss the positives of having a mentor. I raise this issue here because while working with a mentor, it will become apparent when visiting their practice that their communication skills have been refined to a point where the client in a consultation probably does not realise they are being sold to. This is where the skill and experience comes in. Alongside this, if a new practitioner is also undertaking a business course or talking with organisations that can help develop a business plan and strategy, they will all highlight the fact that failure to sell will lead to a business failure.

In the beginning, a new practice will probably not have sufficient funding and resources to help them establish and develop their business. It is at this point we should also discuss leadership skills. For many practitioners like myself who come from a medical background, we do not have to lead a business to continue growth and profits. For most pharmacists, as well as doctors and dentists, in their respective fields, the patients will come to you on a regular basis regardless of where your service is, provided the quality of your service is of good value. However, in the aesthetic field of work, the practitioner plays a larger role in reeling in the clientele.

There are a lot of courses available that will offer a good grounding in business management but these are just the fundamental elements of running a business. These courses will touch on every aspect of running a new business and some will offer specific courses to creating and running a practice similar to yours. This does sound like a lot of new skills to learn but they are all interlinked and easy to pick-up; all that is needed is the ambition and a desire to create a successful and profitable aesthetics practice.

Your training checklist

To help new practitioners there are a number of specialist training firms available to help develop these communication skills and other business skills as well.

Here is my quick checklist of how to find a training company that will help develop your skillset:

- ✓ Ensure that the company is not exclusive to one manufacturer;
- ✓ They need to be independent and offer skills on a variety of treatments and products;
- ✓ Check that the trainers are experts in the procedure they are training in;
- ✓ The professionalism of the company should also be obvious and they should be specialists in their field.

Some of the training firms also offer help with marketing a particular product so it is always worthwhile finding out what they will provide in terms of strategies and documentation.

Manufacturers offer great training opportunities and I have found that most of these sessions are both highly rewarding and informative. Obviously, the major drawback is that the manufacturer is only interested in offering training in their own products which will limit a practitioner's offering to clients. It should also be appreciated that during these training sessions there is little to help people improve how they assess a client's face, for example, and how offering multiple treatments can bring about a desired result.

Finally, there is a big problem within the aesthetics industry whereby people have been setting up a business without any qualifications. There will be legislation to bring this practice to an end but you as future practitioners need to be aware that the person offering the training may be skilled, but they may not have any relevant qualifications or expertise within the industry. You should opt to use training companies and trainers who can prove their qualifications and expertise before parting with any money. I should add also that those without experience within aesthetics are also liable to have bad practice techniques that they may pass on without appreciating just how bad those techniques actually are. After all, practice makes perfect.

Chapter 4
Finding a mentor

For many reasons, finding someone to mentor you could prove very useful. While looking at a training programme to develop various skills and expertise, a mentor can play a pivotal role in your aesthetic skillset and hone your business acumen. Having a mentor means finding time in the week to meet with them; it may mean they come to the practice for one day a week or they meet you at home for one evening, for instance. It may also prove beneficial to spend time within your mentor's practice to see first-hand how their business operates and why they have made it a success.

However, it is not just about learning skills and techniques, it is also observing how they deal with clients, how they promote themselves effectively and how they have developed their business successfully.

I mention communication skills several times in this book because I believe it is very important to leave a lasting impression with a client and it is a good way of offering your professionalism and skills. To be a successful communicator requires a high level of self-awareness and, as with all skills, communication can also be practised and improved upon. I would stress also that a practitioner does not have to alter their communication style with each different client and they should maintain consistency rather than having a chameleon approach.

I was incredibly fortunate to find a mentor in the shape of Dr Vincent Wong who had already established himself as one of the leading aesthetic practitioners within the UK. His client list is impressive and contains a variety of people, including members of the celebrity world. His Harley Street clinic is very popular and busy.

I did not begin my new life as an aesthetic practitioner easily because it was made clear to me from the very beginning that it would not be an easy transition and that it will take time and hard work to build a reputation and create a successful clinic. But I was prepared to take the time and effort to focus on something that I wanted to do. This was quite difficult for my family to appreciate because they saw me work so hard at university to gain my qualifications. My family and friends also had difficulty in understanding why I had left a well-paid job to take a risk with my own business. Having said that, I was working six or seven days a week in a job I did not find rewarding and was unfulfilling. The real secret to my success is that I took a year out of my life to focus on something that I wanted to do and be successful at. I should also mention that when I did have days off as a pharmacist, I would be working in aesthetics and learning more whenever I could. Basically, I was working in a Harley Street clinic for free to develop my skills and learn everything I needed to learn to progress my new career. It is a learning curve and we all have to begin somewhere; all I know is that the beginning of my journey as an aesthetic practitioner began in the world-famous Harley Street with one of the best practitioners around.

This is one of the reasons that I've created a chapter called 'Finding a Mentor' because it's important that you learn from someone who has already made this journey and is willing to share their experience and expertise. While I accept it can be difficult finding a mentor within aesthetics this book will help provide the basics that a mentor may offer. In turn, I'm also a firm believer that by learning from someone above you, you are then obliged to pass on their experience and expertise, as well as your own, to others.

Obviously, I could have set out on my own in the very beginning to establish a clinic and a reputation and I may have made a good success of it. That's a very unlikely scenario because without Dr Wong's help I would have made some serious business errors in the early days which I managed to avoid. For example, I have learnt how to retain clients and how to promote the clinic effectively.

I should also point out that while there are many good business mentors around who are available, I think it is important to find someone who has specific experience in the niche world of aesthetics.

The other question that should be appreciated is to consider how long you will need a mentor for. There are many successful business people who have utilised the experiences of mentors throughout their business career and I would not like to put a definitive timeline on how long you should work with a mentor.

While very few mentors may well offer their time and services for free, a majority of the others will charge a fee. Consideration needs to be taken at this point because someone who is charging will need to contribute to the success of the business and this may be the best route for some who are thinking of setting up a practice.

There are also various business organisations dotted around the UK who will help to set up an arrangement between a mentor and someone looking for mentoring. Indeed, the same business organisation may be able to provide a business angel which is someone who will be willing to invest money in your business venture and offer help and advice to make it a success. Be aware however, that a business angel will also need to take a big percentage of the business's valuation and turnover.

I am also aware that there are people reading this book who would look towards myself or Dr Wong to become their mentors and this is a possibility. Please contact me directly for more details, as Dr Wong and I will be available by telephone and email to provide further information. Our mentoring programme will run for a year and the aim is not to have someone struggling along for the first year but offering real world advice and help and support.

Chapter 5
Choosing your demographic

There are various categories of potential clientele based on age range that the aesthetic practitioner should be looking to attract. For instance, I deal with a lot of people aged between 25 and 40 but the categories cover a much wider client base such as 21 - 25, 40 – 55 and even older than 55.

While some clients may not have a lot of money and they may not invest in your treatments, there are however aesthetic practitioners out there who are not charging a lot for their treatments and who are, in my opinion, undermining the industry.

We will discuss pricing in more detail later in the book but it's important to charge a realistic level that maintains excellence while providing a good level of living standards. For me, my prices compare favourably with those being charged on Harley Street; a rationale for this being that a higher treatment price brings about a higher level of professional and quality service.

Just as a word of advice: should a potential client question your rates and then compare them unfavourably with someone charging less then consider this – the client is essentially paying for the practitioner's experience and expertise. Someone charging £50 for treatment is having to do volume in order to make a living, which means they also have to cut corners; whether it is time, using cheaper products or cheaper premises. You essentially get what you pay for.

I have found from experience the best way to successfully build a clinic is to look at the demographic of those wanting aesthetic treatments which means I aim my services at those aged between 25 – 40 plus. Do not get me wrong, I am also happy treating those within the 21-25-year category but I found most of my clients fall into the 25 – 40-year demographic. This is also the point to mention that my prices reflect my demographic.

It is crucial when developing a practice that the practitioner appreciates market segmentation, which means dividing a customer service and products for a particular segment. This will also affect how you market yourself to potential clients. By segmenting effectively, a practitioner is offering their expertise to meet their client needs; practitioners should also appreciate those needs will vary between age bands and those under 30 – younger clients will probably want treatments that differ from those over 50 for instance.

An efficient way of creating a profitable business is to target clients with large disposable incomes. I have worked for clinics that offer discounted services but the work necessary to produce the required profits means that the days are long and it is hard work. It goes without saying that generally a 25-year-old has less disposable income than someone who is 50 years old and in a profession; therefore, by targeting effectively, the practitioner can charge more and make more profit.

When segmenting a market, a practitioner should be aware that their client base will age, which means their needs for a treatment will develop over time. So, it makes sense to offer treatments that appeal to a particular age group in a bid to retain them as clients, without them switching to rival clinics or competing procedures. The practitioner should also beware the demand for treatments will ebb and flow in popularity, though for many clinics the number one treatment will be anti-wrinkle treatments followed by chemical peels and then dermal fillers.

I will explain later in this book where a new practitioner should set up their clinic and utilise the clients of an already established business, such as a hair salon. There is also the possibility of remaining as a pharmacist and spending one day a week or fortnight with an aesthetics clinic to build-up experience and to determine whether this type of work is what you want to do. I went down this route and found it hugely enjoyable even though it left me with little free time; I was working in the evenings and on Saturdays, but it gave me the knowledge and experience to bring me where I am today.

I appreciate too that there is a temptation for pharmacists who may work in their own business or for a family firm who may try to see clients during their normal working day. I would urge you not to do this simply because in the initial consultation a client will need your undivided attention and I would personally find it difficult switching from delivering prescriptions to then discussing the benefits of dermal fillers.

It may also help to have a business plan that details what your objectives are for the next three to five years. Part of this business plan should detail who your clients are going to be and how you will reach them. It may also help to have a mission statement that spells out clearly and succinctly what you are hoping to achieve in the long run for your business. You could even publish this statement on your website, on promotional literature and in the waiting room of the clinic.

The business plan will also detail how much time and money you will spend on targeting your demographic to attract new clients but the main thing is that the business plan will make you think clearly about how to achieve business success. It will also detail how we will review and quantify that success.

However, a crucial part of the business plan is to determine the market so you will need to decide on your client base, their income, gender and age. If you are not attracting that particular demographic then you need to reassess your marketing activities in a bid to do so. The key here is to be realistic about who you are likely to attract and your treatment prices will also determine this.

There are ways of finding out what the demographic is like in your area and there are specialist firms who will offer low-priced reports on who lives there. These reports will be broken down by gender, status, age, their health and housing type as well as income. The economic activity and ethnicity will also be detailed.

The one thing about a demographic assessment is that it may make you think again as to what treatments you will be offering. For instance, you may be offering muscle relaxants when there is no demand for it from potential clients. However, there may be a demand for chemical peels or mesotherapy.

As part of your demographic research you should also analyse who your competitors are and where they are located. You should also appreciate what their strengths and weaknesses are and how you will effectively compete against them. It cannot all be based on price and therefore customer service will be key to success. You will need to analyse very carefully what competitors are offering and either meet it and/or offer a niche product they do not. It is always worthwhile to see how they market themselves and to see what they specialise in.

To summarise, I have mentioned earlier in this chapter about being careful with your treatment pricing when starting out a new aesthetics practice because you need to make a living, however you might be fortunate to attract a demographic that is happy to pay for quality and an impressive level of service. Again, careful thought should be given to who you are targeting and what they are prepared to pay.

Chapter 6

Procedure pricing

From the very beginning anyone starting out as an aesthetic practitioner, will need to appreciate that they do not have to offer the widest possible range of treatments to potential clients and instead should focus on a client's needs and then focus on the pricing levels.

Many practitioners believe they must provide a wide range of aesthetic treatments in a bid to beat their competitors, but this is not the case. It is also important to appreciate that many 'new' treatments are not new at all, but simply a duplication or an innovative approach to an existing treatment. To my mind, a practice that offers a long list of treatments does not appreciate their client's needs or the market itself. Practitioners should spend time identifying their market rather than offering everything and hoping that the market comes to them.

This is important because specialising in a treatment will pay dividends and it would be difficult to maintain this level of expertise for every treatment and product that is available. By developing one's expertise, a practitioner will grow their reputation and help build-up a loyal client base. It is also a better way to gain publicity in magazines in the health and beauty market as well as establishing credentials.

A practitioner's decision on what they will offer to the client should not be influenced by the latest trends or what clients have read in a magazine. It should instead, be influenced by their strengths of carrying out a treatment. A practitioner should never begin delivering a new treatment to clients solely based on the recommendation of a sales representative from a major product manufacturer. A detailed knowledge base should be developed from in-depth research around this new product before one decides to adopt and deliver the treatment.

Another important point worth bearing in mind is that many clients approaching practitioners are doing so because they have read magazine articles and suchlike which promise fantastic results with a treatment. Practitioners should be diligent and explain that the results they see may not be the same as those they read about and that because their face is different from the face featured in the article.

This will mean having the necessary communication skills to discuss these matters effectively with a client so they appreciate exactly what they should be expecting and it's also important that should a client come for a consultation and ask for a treatment the practitioner thinks unsuitable, then they should explain so. We must live with the fact that in the real world many clients who are turned down for treatment will simply go to another practitioner who will be willing to accept their money; as I have stressed before ethics is a crucial part of our business approach and helps to set us apart from our rivals.

One important element for establishing a pricing structure for the offered treatments is to not only understand and appreciate the target market, but also to help deliver your own personal and business financial objectives. All new businesses need a plan to establish themselves within a marketplace and to ensure they make enough profit to sustain and grow the business. It may be that a practitioner wants to develop their business slowly, which may mean increasing turnover by 10% every year. They may decide to develop their business by retaining clients because a client who spends regularly is going to be a good source of income and you do not have to spend money in recruiting them. Another way to develop profitability for a practice is to increase how much a client spends in their visit. This is where communication skills and learning how to upsell other products will be key.

Essentially, the practitioner will need to lay out the financial objectives they want to achieve which will influence their procedure prices. To help determine what the prices should be, there are two levels of objectives to consider.

The first level is to consider the practice and where you want your business to be within a year, after 24 months and 36 months. Many new businesses set out with a five-year plan and this could be a useful tool when setting out because it gives you landmarks to aim for on your path to success.

The next level is to breakdown the practice functions and set objectives for each of these. As an example, if you want to increase turnover by 10% in your second year of operation then you will need to determine where that turnover will come from. By this time, you will have discovered which treatments bring most profit, which are the most popular and which could generate more money for you. It may be that you have a figure in mind and so this means increasing turnover for each of the functions to deliver the top line aim.

It is at this point we should mention the SMART criteria, which many people will be aware of but can prove useful when setting objectives for the business.

Specific: be specific about what the objective of your business is going to be and stick to it.

Measurable: at any point in your business plan you should be able to evaluate how you are performing against your list of objectives. Each of these objectives should be measurable so you can determine which are being more successful than others.

Achievable: we must always be realistic about the business targets we set ourselves because if they are not achievable they will simply deter us from reaching our objectives and prove to be a disincentive.

Relevant: all of the stated objectives should have a relevance to those who are responsible for achieving them. In the first year, most of this responsibility will be yours so you can relate to what needs to be done so when you come to employ people or share objectives then they need to take responsibility for this.

Time bound: When setting out your SMART objectives you should also set yourself a realistic deadline that means your objectives can be achieved. These are the landmarks I mentioned earlier and you should measure your progress against these, particularly when it comes to attracting new clients, profitability and turnover.

All businesses have a financial forecast and have a plan on how to market themselves and achieve their financial aims for the coming year. I do know of medical and pharmacy practices that do not have similar plans and simply work on a day-to-day basis. The main reason for this is that their business simply 'walks in through the door' and so a certain level of turnover is guaranteed. While this creates a comfort zone, it also means that pharmacists, particularly, who decide to create their own business have then to learn how to plan for business success and gear their efforts towards achieving their objectives. Many medical professionals will be unable to do this but there are tools and help around to assist them.

As an example, I would suggest that a pharmacist who is giving up the regular income of either working for a major chain or working as a locum should aim to earn around £5,500 per month. This is a realistic financial target and one that can be achieved within the first year of operating. If we break that figure down it will take around 20 hours every month to reach it. To do this, the practitioner will need five clients per week - so this would be the consultation time, as well as a total of five treatments per week including the selling of additional treatments to at least one of those clients. This is a nice base to start from and in the second year, the practitioner should be aiming to double the number of clients they are seeing or, at the very least, growing the number of profitable treatments they carry out. It is also important to have a high retention rate - though no one will achieve 100% because that is the nature of the business.

By using the SMART criteria, a practitioner will have a road map to success. It will give them a clear idea of what they need to do on an annual, quarterly, monthly, weekly and a daily basis. Without a plan, the business will inevitably struggle but it does not have to be this way. The real secret to having a business plan is to check it on a regular basis and ensure that the measurable objectives are being met. If they are not being met, then action needs to be taken for the business to meet its overall objectives. This may mean recruiting more new clients or carrying out more profitable treatments. The main aim is to get back onto the roadmap to success and by not checking progress on a regular basis the practitioner may be a long way off achieving their first year aims. It should go without saying that by having a year-end assessment, one will be able to identify what the problems are and how they can be resolved.

Over the course of a year there will be repeat business from the clients and I would aim to achieve a retention rate of 70-80%. If this figure is not being reached, then you need to address the problems that may be leading to this; it may mean that your people skills need polishing or there is something lacking in the consultation phase. It may also mean that they are not happy with their treatment, which could lead to them not speaking highly of your services to their friends and family.

I would also refer to my business plan to determine which of my treatments is the most popular and which is the most profitable. I would analyse their uptake on a monthly basis and consider why one month is better than the other. It may simply be that your marketing efforts were more successful in one month and, if so, you should look at what you did and repeat it.

Essentially, by having a business plan we can fix any problem quickly to achieve our overall aims. The other big plus for having a business plan is for when we employ others or work with freelancers; the plan will help explain what your business is about, who your clients are, how you reach those clients and what treatments you deliver. You can also explain and inspire your colleagues about the efficacy of the plan and how crucial communication is within the business and to the clients. The plan is also important for staff because a drop in one type of treatment may be simply down to the poor follow-up process conducted by a member of staff. If that is the case, then they need training or supervising more closely to ensure that they reach their own targets.

I do hate clichés but this is an important one to remember: if you fail to plan, then you are planning to fail.

Chapter 7
Choosing suppliers

For anyone setting up a new aesthetics practice it will soon become clear that there are a lot of suppliers in the industry; many of them are good but some of them are not. There are many different manufacturers of dermal fillers, for instance, and dozens who make micro-dermabrasion equipment and a huge number of skin-care companies.

All of these firms and organisations will claim that they are the very best at what they do and their products are leading the market. As with any offering, the practitioner should treat each of these claims with care. It is also important that a practitioner does not use too many suppliers and instead uses a key supplier for a treatment.

When I say that care is needed, the practitioner should look to see how long the manufacturer has been in business and what the reputation of its products are. A key question to ask here is, "Do they have a successful track record and have they ever had problems with any of their products?"

Some manufacturers will also supply marketing materials and these can be very useful. It is always worth checking to see whether they will provide marketing support or any support for their products. Most of these manufacturers invest in their own marketing channels and, as a result, this strategy may lead to clients being attracted to your business. Do not lose sight of the fact that the use of a product may affect your own business reputation, so do not be shy about asking for customer testimonials from manufacturers.

Judging a potential supplier on the knowledge and professionalism of their representatives is vital. What you are looking for here is whether the manufacturer can add a value to the business and help make it a success.

In some clinics there will need to be an investment in equipment but this does not have to be a capital investment since most equipment can be leased. This will mean that the initial outlay will be much lower and profitability higher. Perhaps the most effective way, and this also works for promotion purposes, is to team up with someone who has the equipment required such as laser instruments which are commonly used for procedures such as laser hair removal or pigmentation improvement. This is something that I currently do for one of my own clinics and our partnership works extremely well. I have clients that need laser hair removal which I pass onto my colleague and she likewise has clients wanting aesthetic treatments that she passes on to me.

When it comes to finding the suppliers for treatments it is necessary to appreciate that there are hundreds, if not thousands of these products available so you will need to breakdown what kind of treatment you will be offering and who will be the best supplier.

In aesthetics, these categories would cover things like volumisers, muscle relaxants, skin texturing, topical and bio-stimulation.

Topical treatments can help reverse sun damage and treat acne as well as reducing the appearance of wrinkles. Before signing up with a manufacturer it is always worth checking the product's ingredients and that the price of the product will help deliver healthy profits.

As an example, the most popular ingredients for cosmeceuticals are vitamin C or ascorbic acid which is one of the essential factors for the formation and function of healthy collagen. It also provides daytime protection as an antioxidant and will protect the skin from harmful sun rays and damaging free radicals.

Vitamin E: This is another popular ingredient since it helps smooth the skin and prevents premature ageing. It does this by blocking lipid peroxidation which damages cell membranes in tissue.

Vitamin B5: all living cells have B5 in them and it helps in the synthesis of proteins, lipids and carbohydrates. Indeed, many dermatological disorders are caused by deficiencies in B5.

Hyaluronic acid: products that contain hyaluronic acid will benefit the skin. It is an efficient water buffer and binder as well as an antioxidant. Clients should be reminded that they will need strong sun protection in addition to using this product.

Lactic acid: also known as alpha hydroxyl acid it is an effective naturally occurring humectant in our skin. In cases of hyperkeratosis, it has been shown that lactic acid can reduce excessive epidermal keratinisation. Products with lactic acid can be used both day and night since the product is a polyhydroxy acid. Products with this ingredient can be used at night for the hydration of dehydrated skin. Clients who use lactic acid products during the day will need sunblock. Indeed, to protect from harmful sun rays and free radicals, a practitioner should also include Vitamin A and Vitamin C as antioxidants.

Squalane: an important part of the functioning of the lipid system is squalane which occurs naturally in human skin. As an active ingredient it treats dry skin and can be used for both day and night care though some protection will be needed for daytime use.

Retinol: acts quickly to diminish the appearance of wrinkles and fine lines by accelerating the skin's natural exfoliation process. Retin A (a Vitamin A treatment) can improve skin imperfections and tone since it's an effective exfoliate.

Salicylic acid: For patients with acne, salicylic acid is a proven antibacterial destroying agent though for daytime use, clients will need to use sun protection.

Canella Asiatica: hard to find in stores because it has a short shelf life, canella asiatica is an agent that increases collagen production. Helps to reduce the appearance of stretch marks.

Glycolic acid: as a natural fruit acid, glycolic acid helps to produce vibrant and younger-looking skin by improving circulation. The product helps to accelerate the skin's cellular turnover.

Sodium hyalurate: for help in making skin appear soft, silky smooth and supple, sodium hyaluronite works as a lubricant between the skin's connective tissues.

For many reasons, choosing a supplier is crucial because of the different client's treatment requirements. Indeed, a client's needs will differ depending on their skin damage and age. So, while most clients are sensitive to the cost of the treatment, it makes for good business practice to have a variety of treatment types and prices on offer, so that some treatments will provide much larger profit margins while other treatments will not. Do not be afraid to 'mix and match' between suppliers despite what a sales representative might say.

However, the real secret to delivering top quality skin care to clients is not about understanding what the products will do but diagnosing correctly a client's needs from their skin condition. An appreciation of cosmeceutical ingredients is important but knowing how to apply them correctly more so.

Many clients will approach a practitioner wanting that elixir that will prevent them from ageing but most ingredients contained in products available will help to slow down that ageing process while improving the skin's condition to look rejuvenated and youthful.

Earlier I mentioned a growing demand from clients wanting to look younger, if not prevent the ageing process. One of the most popular treatments now being offered by many practitioners is for chemical peels. These are effective and carry good profit margins too. I will explain briefly what some of the peels are.

Alpha hydroxyl acids are found in fruits and plants and have been used as moisturisers for hundreds of years. However, over the last 10 years the use of these products has grown to include the treatment for sun damaged skin, acne, fine wrinkles and pigmented skin.

When it comes to offering a treatment, the alpha hydroxyl acid will remove the thick layer of dead skin cells which cover the surface of the skin. This layer often has the complexion of a dull appearance and when the acid is used regularly it will lift the dead skin cells to leave the client with a rejuvenated and healthy appearance. It also appears that the acids help to stimulate new cell growth which over a course of treatments will help give the appearance of tightened and more youthful skin.

While there are many products with this ingredient available in creams, lotions and cleansers as well as sunscreens and gels, they are popular for home hygiene routines. However, alpha hydroxy acid peels in their more concentrated solution can only be applied within a practice by a trained practitioner. Depending on the client's skin type, the solution is applied by the practitioner to the client's skin and left for a period of time and then washed off or neutralised. The upper layers of the skin will then peel away over the coming days and the beauty of the treatment is that the client will not have to stop doing regular activities. These are light peels and the client may need several treatments before the desired result is achieved.

The market for skin peels is a competitive one for suppliers and I would urge practitioners not to choose a particular skin peel based on cost. You should ensure that the treatments you carry out deliver the expected results. I would also urge practitioners not to choose a cheap skin peel while charging top prices also. It's always best to over-deliver on a client's expectations because then you will have a happy client who you will see on a regular basis and who will be happy to recommend your services.

TCA peels: practitioners also have the chance to use trichloroacetic acid, or TCA peels. Again, these can only be applied by a trained practitioner on their premises and have a deeper peeling effect than is seen from alpha hydroxy acids. These peels can improve a wide range of conditions including freckling, sun damage, weathered skin, shallow acne scars and pigmentation.

Practitioners must pay careful attention to how long the peel stays on the skin and it is then washed off or neutralised. Clients will say they can feel a burning sensation but that is the peel taking effect. When removed, the TCA peel will take with it the skin's upper layers which will then dry and peel off over the coming days though a client they appear to have sunburn they will not have to take time off work and will need to apply moisturisers. The end result is a new layer of healthier skin.

We should also mention dermal fillers and there are three categories of them. The first of these are biodegradable products which break down over time. The average for a how long a treatment lasts for will depend on the individual and the areas that have been treated. Most of treatments will last for around six to nine months but most of the treatments are affordable and are growing in popularity.

The next category of dermal fillers are semi-permanent ones. These last longer than the biodegradable ones and are particularly useful should practitioner want to add volume to the client's lower face or cheekbones.

The third category is for permanent dermal fillers. I would suggest that practitioners, particularly those who are new to aesthetics, are careful with permanent products because success in their use is not guaranteed. In addition, as the client ages then their use of permanent products may become obvious and so the treatment may not suit them over a long period of time.

Mesotherapy: this is an increasingly popular treatment that sees a client receiving injections into their subcutaneous fat of vitamins, plant extracts, pharmaceuticals and herbs. Mesotherapy is aimed at facial rejuvenation and provides a series of treatments to allow for better protein construction while vitamins provide for deficiencies. Unlike some treatments, mesotherapy has a cumulative effect as the body will develop elastin and collagen over time with between two and four treatments taking place every two or three weeks. Essentially, this is a revitalising treatment and clients will see an improvement in the texture, hydration and tone of their skin after their first treatment.

One popular use for mesotherapy is for cellulite and fat reduction. There is a specific formula of nutrients that will help with cellulite treatments and clients will see improved lymphatic and venous circulation. The treatment will dissolve fat lobules that are trapped in connectivity tissue bands and help create a smoother, tighter surface of skin; the dimpled look that cellulite brings will also be removed.

When it comes to fat reduction, mesotherapy works in a similar way as it does with ridding the body of cellulite.

One of the inevitable questions that will arise from new practitioners and established ones alike is, "Which are the current most popular aesthetic treatments available?". This is one reason why practitioners should identify which treatments are growing in the market and then establish who the main suppliers of those products are. There is no doubt that the sales representatives of the manufacturers will be in regular contact and will offer the latest products and information on how they can be used to help grow your business.

Chapter 8

Negotiation skills

The topic of negotiation skills may appear to be a strange one to add to a book about starting up an aesthetics practice, but it is very important.

I mention this because I look to my father who is very good at negotiating and he is forever getting discounts on just about everything he can, simply by negotiating with the person selling. However, negotiation skills will be paramount when negotiating with the salon or the gym you may find your clinic based within. It's not simply about negotiating with potential clients, it's about using opportunities of working with other businesses to develop your own. Part of this will mean having to decide whether you are going to pay rent or work on a percentage of the clinic's turnover within a salon, for example.

In addition, it is also important to have negotiation skills for when a client comes into the clinic and they may not know the first thing about you or the treatments you offer. This means having to sell you and your business offering to them to the very best of your ability. It is important to reach their 'key triggers' so that they like you and trust you. It is also important to appreciate that the client will want to be safe when being treated. If your negotiation skills are not up to scratch, then a potential client will simply walk out and go to another rival clinic to get the treatment they are looking for.

I have given this chapter the title 'negotiating skills' because I think it covers a broad range of subjects that aesthetic practitioners really need to get to grips with. On the one hand, we do need to be friendly and outgoing, whilst on the other hand we need confidence in selling our skills and expertise while offering the treatments at a realistic price to a potential client.

One of my clinics is in a very popular hairdressing salon in London and I get on well with the staff, so I have mentioned to them that I would consider offering them treatments if they then told their clients about where they got their treatment from and how impressed they were with it. This will also encourage word-of-mouth to help promote the business and is simply another way to reach out to clients.

We should also consider that the development of negotiation skills is also about developing one's self-confidence. I appreciate that not everyone is happy negotiating or bartering but if you are setting out in business there are things that you must do to enable a business to become the success you want it to be. Learning negotiation skills and then utilising those skills will pay dividends.

While there are courses available to develop such skillsets, I personally have never undertaken any myself. I have simply decided to negotiate whenever I can, as it is something that comes naturally to me. I grew up watching my father practising it and it is also something that I enjoy. A large part of a successful negotiation is to be confident and know what your limits are when discussing prices.

However, others who may need some tips and directions here is some helpful advice; it's important to understand that everyone can improve their negotiation skills which will see a growth in sales.

Firstly, always make sure that you understand and appreciate what the other person is looking for. There's no point a client coming for a personal consultation about a skin peel, for instance, and you try to sell them a completely different treatment. Always listen and try to deliver to their expectations.

Next, it's important that you should not be side-tracked by the client and always remain focused on the issues to be negotiated; this means not discussing the weather, for instance, but discussing potential aesthetic treatments.

Another important tip when conducting negotiations is to find out how the client will define a successful treatment so this means understanding the outcomes they are wanting. It may mean this is a good opportunity for selling other add-on treatments for the client to achieve the outcome they are looking for.

I've mentioned previously that confidence is very important when negotiating and discussing treatments with a client so you should be assertive but not aggressively so and when offering a solution to a client's needs, do not use a weak voice which will enable a client to enter the discussion and either turn down a treatment or negotiate on the price.

Just to underline the level of confidence is not just about the voice, a lot of confidence is about body language so you will need to make eye contact and display confidence.

Another trick to help reinforce a selling point is to use silence which will enable the client to think about the offer and it also means they do not appear to be rushed into making a decision. Having silences at crucial moments mean you will remain in control of the personal consultation without losing ground.

Finally, it's important that once the negotiations are complete that the intended treatments and the costs for it are written down so there's no misunderstanding about what is being offered and what the potential cost for that treatment will be. Another reason for writing down a client's needs and treatments is that it is more difficult to change the consultation agreement afterwards.

It should also be appreciated by any pharmacist looking to enter the aesthetics industry is that we are all, whether we like it or whether we realise it or not are involved in selling. At some point, we need to sell our skills to a potential employer and regardless of what we do for a living, most of us will be selling something at some point - it may be selling the positive reasons for a new project to an employer, for instance, but it still means dictating how the negotiations are conducted.

Of course, the best salesman and women are the ones who can sell without the client or customer realising that they are being sold to; this is simply about confidence and using language effectively to control a conversation and to negotiate effectively.

There may be some pharmacists reading this who believe they may lack the confidence to do this but they will have experience of dealing with patients already and negotiation with a client is a vital part of making an aesthetic practice the success you deserve.

Chapter 9
Internal/external promotion

The most important issue to remember when contemplating how to promote a new aesthetics practice to potential clients is that we are looking to build-up a relationship by offering a quality service at a good price. While marketing itself involves several elements including planning, advertising and management - for a practitioner setting up, the main focus should be on identifying the needs of potential clients and then developing the necessary services and products to meet our client's needs.

If your new practice is well-funded and you have enough money to employ someone to help you run it, or it takes off and is an early success and you are contemplating employing people, then you need to appreciate that new employees need to focus on this client relationship so the level of customer service remains high and the client remains happy. Let us not lose sight of the fact that happy clients mean that they will return again and again which means more profit without having to spend money on marketing our practice to new clients.

It is always worthwhile offering promotions in a bid to attract and retain clients. There are two common routes that an aesthetics practice can explore in order to promote their business. The first being the Public Relations (PR) route, which will help grow your business by strategically exposing the company to its potential clientele and to also build a beneficial relationship between the two parties. This is often done via the recruitment of a PR agency or individuals who specialise in the promotion of aesthetics. The second route is self-promotion of one's business by approaching different media platforms such promotional websites, newspapers and magazines that help to attract clientele via discount offers for treatments and products.

Initially, I used PR to establish my practice and to attract clients. I was spending a small fortune every month and it did work to a limited extent. For instance, I appeared in a Sky TV documentary on aesthetics and I appeared in a few articles on the subject too. For anyone thinking of using a PR agency I should warn you that it does take time for PR to work, it is not going to be an overnight success because media does not work in that way. It will take time and real effort using PR to establish oneself as an expert and build-up your client base. So, while I used PR over the short term and then decided to stop using the agency, I believe that I will return to them in a bid to position myself within the market more effectively.

One such example of a self-promoting platform is *'Wowcher';* a website that is used to attract clients to companies by offering discounts for their products and services. While this may generate income in the short term, it tends not to provide a reliable flow of clients because the promotion means that the clients may only be attracted to the company solely based on the lower and temporary price being offered.

While on the subject of promotion, we really should mention 'Search Engine Optimisation' (SEO) - which is a part of having an effective web presence. It also means utilising the power of social media, which is becoming increasingly important in our daily lives and reach out to potential clients, though for many practitioners this may be a time-consuming and what appears to be a fruitless task. I would urge you to stick with it.

It is also possible to hire SEO experts to undertake this work on your behalf, though this may cost quite a lot and there is no guarantee of success. Most agencies will offer an analysis to show that the social media work has been improved and delivered real results. Most people setting up their aesthetics practice may not realise that SEO also extends to the words that you use to describe your work and yourself on the website. This means using 'keywords' effectively within your own website, which is a way to incorporate the terms that people are searching for. This allows the search engines to understand and appreciate what your website is about and then deliver people looking for that service.

In the first week of operations, I attracted more than 100 followers to my social media accounts which means people were interested in me and what I was offering. This also means that followers are often willing to retweet or repost offers and promotions as well as news and advice.

Practitioners should appreciate that their marketing efforts will need to differ if they are targeting the female market rather than the male market. Adverts tailored for use in women's magazines will, obviously, be of no use to be published in a men's magazine. This means it also makes sense to have different parts of your clinic's website detailing specific female treatments and another section for male treatments. You will also need to produce brochures that cover everything and have literature that is specific to male and female clients.

There is one little trick that all practitioners can do and that is to target a specific treatment towards a specific section of your intended market. Do not try to market your services in their entirety within a marketing push, since the message will be lost on your target audience. Instead, it makes better sense to target a specific treatment to a specific market, for instance offering skin treatments to women aged over 50 and when they are sat in front of you then offer other treatments that you believe will be suitable for them. These extra treatments – called 'up-selling' - could include muscle relaxants, dermal fillers and even laser hair removal. This same tactic also applies to the male market.

In addition, while the majority of clients are women and the market itself is growing at a phenomenal rate currently, there is also a rapidly increasing market for men too. Practitioners will inevitably find that men have been sent to the clinic by their wives for treatment and they may not be entirely sure of what they want. As with all consultations, the treatment must be suitable to the client rather than a way to boost profitability. Ethics is a crucial part of our work.

An important part of choosing which segment of the market a practitioner is going to aim for and make a success of will also influence the use of hiring a specialist PR agency. For many people setting out to become aesthetic practitioners, this could be an expensive outlay to begin with but may (depending on the target market) be money well spent. When I began as a practitioner I used a very good PR agency and I negotiated on their rate so it was more in line with my budget. They did some very good things initially and I was getting mentioned in magazines and there was some interest from potential clients. However, the interest from these potential clients were not 'qualified leads' so I had to put in extra effort to sell them my services and treatments. After a few months I decided to stop my PR campaign and invest the budget elsewhere to effectively promote my clinic.

There is no doubt that the use of PR to boost the profile of a clinic can be money well spent but the media world has changed in recent years so the PR message can easily get lost. As a result the campaign itself needs to be very focused and direct and well supported. Do not forget that you will need to advertise and that some magazines can be very expensive to place adverts in. Unless you already have an established reputation, the expense for promotion and marketing is one that needs to be made and it needs to be effective.

It should also be remembered that the money spent on PR may well be spent more profitably on SEO, since the majority of potential new clients will do their research online before making contact. As your clinic grows, then the word-of-mouth recommendations will begin and success will be yours.

One important tip for anyone starting out with a new aesthetics clinic is that the work of promotion is not something you just do at the very beginning; it is something that is vital to the success of a business and needs to be maintained and carried out on a regular basis. Whether this means undertaking frequent PR campaigns to target different segments of the market, it is something that needs to be done. It is also important that the website is updated on a regular basis as this is what search engines want to see, so consider having a blog which details the ongoing success of the business and to highlight the practitioner's own expertise in delivering excellent levels of treatment.

Another effective route to promote a new practice is to work with somebody who already has a spa, salon or gym as they will also have a client base and a promotional budget. By using an associate, a pharmacist could develop a business plan which utilises these business premises. The business owner will either charge a rent or a percentage of the profits being made. Some businesses will ask for both and this is where your newfound negotiation skills will pay dividends!

It is always best to set up a trial first so you can appreciate how much profit you will make from the leads that the business provides. Obviously, if the associated business generates a lot of client enquiries (which you can then turn into paid-for treatments), then you should reward the associate accordingly so you have a positive relationship and they remain committed to delivering clients to your practice.

I have worked with some excellent business associates who have worked hard on my behalf so I can highly recommend this to establish a practice quickly and effectively. It will mean, however, if your practice is based within a salon that you will need to educate the people who work there about the treatments being offered. It may mean that you offer free or discounted treatments to the staff, so that they can then give first-hand accounts to their own clients and recommend you as well. By establishing a practice in a popular hair salon or gym, for instance, you are targeting a part of the market that is making an effort with their appearance and they would automatically be interested in other ways to look good. A practitioner should stress to the people working in the salon that they would be offering a valuable service to their clients and that this would be an integrated service.

Many of these locations also have a very good receptionist team and it is always worth bearing in mind that they are the first point of call for new clients. It may be a good idea to offer incentives for them to publicise your business and to attract clients that way. A good receptionist can also schedule appointments and make any follow-up calls and also offer a welcome greeting and offer them consent forms and information.

For those practitioners who would like to start a business in this way you will need to consider which treatments are being offered because you will need a variety to make a good profit. Not everyone is after dermal fillers and a practice that focuses just on those treatments will struggle to fill their appointment diary.

There is also the opportunity of starting a practice with another clinic by renting within their premises. This is also a good idea since they will also have the infrastructure in place such as having a receptionist to answer telephone calls and make appointments. The clinic will also have their own marketing activity.

Another idea for a practitioner setting out is to work from home and while this may be a good long-term business plan there will be hefty capital set-up costs as well as the issue of promoting the business, since this will be your responsibility. Also, not everyone wants to have a treatment in their practitioner's home.

The bottom line for these options, is that client generation is the secret to business success. This part of creating a practice will take longer than many envisage and will probably cost more money too. Indeed, it may take a year or more to establish a new practice, depending on how much free time you have to commit to the project before launching, which is why many pharmacists coming from an NHS background prefer to work with business associates who already have a large client base. While working with an associate will make a dent in profitability, it is also the easiest and quickest way to establish a practice.

There is no doubt for a pharmacist who is considering a future in aesthetics that working with an associate is a sensible route.

Setting a marketing budget as well as a marketing plan is an important part of the work we need to do. When we talk about marketing, what we are saying is that we understand the sector we are working in and we understand our client's needs and desires. While this may sound simple and trite, it is not at all.

While marketing is not an easy discipline to learn, there is a lot that a practitioner can do. Remember, it is not always about advertising your treatments, the rejuvenating of a person's look and giving them a confidence boost is also just as important. A further advantage of regular marketing is that it reminds your current clients how good you are and it also means that new practitioners to aesthetics will find it more difficult to attract your clients to their business.

There is no need to over-analyse the market to determine where new business is, but to be honest about your service offering and meet client demands. Again, this goes hand-in-glove with the business plan I mentioned earlier in the book because the marketing plan will help ensure that the business's objectives are met. There are marketing courses available to new businesses and I would recommend them because they give the basics and a good understanding of what a business needs to do and how they can do it without having to employ expensive specialists.

Of course, as your business develops, you will create your own client database that will consist of clients you have treated and of potential clients who have shown an interest in what you do. All of your marketing activities, whether it is by email or brochure, should be aimed at those people in the first instance because they will provide the most cost-effective way of generating business.

Another effective way of attracting new clients is to stage regular seminars on your premises which are informal meetings but they are a great way to find potential clients because they have expressed an interest in the treatment and then spent time learning more about them from you. This will mean having to develop a presentation that sells your skills and expertise to the public and it is always worthwhile rehearsing it as much as you can and practice your presentation in front of family and friends.

If you are working as a pharmacist and have a clear idea of when you will leave pharmacy to begin as an aesthetic practitioner, then you need to work on your marketing plan many months before setting up a business. It is a good idea to have clients lined-up ready and waiting but in practice this may not be possible.

As a guide, from day one the practitioner should have their website up and running, promotional literature available including business cards and plans to hold seminars or at least give presentations in other locations such as popular gyms. You will also need to go out and meet business owners to build a relationship with them and create the possibility of holding a clinic on their premises.

Many people starting out are probably thinking of advertising in local newspapers and magazines but, from my experience, this can be an expensive mistake to make since they do not generate enough new clients to cover the cost of the advert. I would recommend spending money on marketing your website online to attract clients instead.

Finally, the one thing to remember about a marketing plan is that it is not designed to generate profits but purely to generate client interest. Once you have a potential client interested in your services and treatments then all of your other business skills such as selling, consultation and negotiation as well as people management and telephone skills will help bring the profits.

This chapter of internal and external promotion is quite long because it is a crucial element to delivering new clients to your business. The most effective way to promote a business is from client referral because word-of-mouth is invaluable advertising.

Many new aesthetics practices will spend a small fortune on advertising their services in local newspapers and in the Yellow Pages or yell.com. This may be a successful tactic but the truth is that by advertising alone you are too reliant on one medium which, if it fails, will fail to deliver the necessary number of new clients. It is also worth bearing in mind that as the aesthetics sector becomes increasingly competitive that your rivals will also be advertising in the same publications and so your message will be lost. This means you will need a broader range of promotional activity to generate awareness of your business. I have already highlighted the potential of working with other businesses such as a salon or gym but practitioners can also host seminars and then use loyalty programs to help with client retention. Some may also find that direct mail may also boost the number of enquiries but this could be expensive. Once you have become established, it is important to have regular newsletters that may contain news of client promotions. Newsletters are often put to the bottom of a to-do list by practitioners but they are an excellent way to communicate and can be used for future PR purposes as well as being published on the website. When writing a newsletter, highlight the latest aesthetic treatments and client offerings and any new treatments that are on offer. It also makes sense to offer a money off voucher that can be detached from the newsletter or printed from the website for a particular treatment. Again, ensure that there is a time limit on the offer.

Always remember to set a time limit on any client offering. This is also the time when web marketing becomes more important and this will also include utilising social media.

One other aspect for client promotion is to have current clients recommend their friends or family and being rewarded for doing so. If they do recommend a friend, then have them give a card stating that they have been referred. It may also prove beneficial to offer gift certificates to be used at the practice.

On top of this effort, there is also an excellent opportunity for all practitioners to utilise their waiting room to help with their soft selling. This means that while a client is waiting for a consultation they can be reading promotional literature or even watch a promotional film on a flatscreen TV. It should also be appreciated that the waiting room should be a very pleasant place to be in and should be well decorated and carefully designed. Also, have a binder of client testimonials to hand and it may also help to offer free Wi-Fi so the client can work while they wait.

If you have been particularly successful in your PR strategy and been featured in newspapers or magazines or in any online publication, then have these printed out and either put into frames to place on the wall or put into a binder. These positive articles will help sell the practitioner's expertise and treatments. It is always worthwhile remembering that any soft promotion should be low-key and should not dominate the waiting area.

Chapter 10

Web development

The subject of web development has deliberately been placed late in the course of this book's contents because careful thought needs to be given to a website for many reasons. Firstly, it's a shop window for your business and they are easy to create, though investing in a web developer may be money well spent if the website is easy to update without their involvement. Secondly, most new clients begin their search for a treatment online and so they need to find your business quickly and easily.

I would highlight the fact that it is at this point that the aesthetic practitioner decides on a business name and on a suitable logo. Obviously, practitioners may decide to use their own name in the business title, which is an effective way for self-promotion.

I would also urge anyone starting out to consider having a logo for their business created as this can be used on the website and on their literature. This is an effective way of branding and helps clients and potential clients remember who you are. Logos can be created using simple software programs or by using a specialist.

A website is also important because it will contain your promotional material and help sell your business and your professionalism in delivering quality treatments. Some websites will also enable a client to book an appointment online and this could prove very useful, if you do not have a receptionist or you do not want to get involved in 'email ping-pong' with a potential client.

As part of the web development, careful thought needs to be given to the site's content. We mention elsewhere in the book how important it is to target a market segment and to write specifically for male and female clients. It is also important because search engines will need to understand what your site is about and so there will need to be extensive use of keywords, those are the terms people use to search to find websites like yours. A web developer will be fully aware of the need to meet the criteria.

The Internet has moved on in recent years so it is not just a case of having a website and leaving it hoping that people will find it. The website needs to be promoted and it needs to be regularly updated. Obviously, you can hire professionals to do this for you but it's just as easy to do it yourself.

The main reason for having a website is that it becomes a shop window for the practice and enables potential clients to see what you can do and how well you do it. You need to give a good impression so use effective photographs for this purpose.

When we discuss website promotion, what we mean is that when people use a search engine to find an aesthetics practice in the area, they are sent to your website and not to a rival's site instead. At the very least, you should have strong branding of your site and give a clear idea of what you do. It is also important to have your business location and hours of operation stated clearly - if you open at weekends then stress this. Potential clients should be able to contact you easily so have the phone number at the top of the website and give visitors the chance to contact you by email also. Remember to check your inbox regularly and respond quickly to these queries.

One of the strongest parts to the website should be any public relations material, and don't be shy about using anything about you that has appeared in media such as newspapers and magazines as this this will help sell you as an expert in your field.

Along with a list of treatments should be a glossary of terms to explain what words mean and what the treatment will do. It may be a good idea to use photographs from before and after client treatments (though it would be wise to obtain patient consent before doing so) and offer a location with a map showing where you are.

The practitioner's own qualifications and experience are very important elements to establish, so state what they are as well as any accreditations and have several photographs of you and your staff on the site. I would also stress that having client testimonials will also be important as is having news and events so people can see what you have done or are planning to do.

I have mentioned before that you can hire web developers and they will be willing to update the website on a regular basis but this is money you could save if you update the site yourself; most websites, particularly if they are WordPress sites are easy to maintain and manage. It is also important that the website is easy for a visitor to use and can be navigated clearly. One overlooked aspect for web development is that the pages should load quickly and, this is increasingly important for clients and for search engines alike, the pages should also work well on a variety of devices such as mobile phones and tablets.

Promoting your website online is quite straightforward and will mean having to register it with search engines so that they know you exist and can deliver traffic. The most effective way of attracting clients is to optimise the site which is to use the keywords that people are searching for and these should be incorporated within your website's content.

There is also the opportunity of using directories, which will create a link to your site while others may decide to use adverts and sponsored links. This means creating a banner for use on other sites and this may be a fruitful opportunity.

However, perhaps the most effective way of promoting a website business online, particularly if it is a new business, is to use Google AdWords. These are the adverts that appear on top of any search engine results. Depending on the words being paid for, this can be an expensive way to promote your business but they can be successful and so if you attract a large number of client queries, this could be a cost-effective way of building up your business quickly.

Again, how your website operates is an important element of business today so you need to regularly analyse its effectiveness and decide whether more money needs to be spent on promotion or whether you need a more effective website. This may appear to be a time-consuming task but it will be time well spent since, as I mentioned before, most clients now begin their search online so you need to have a web presence and it needs to detail exactly what you can do for them.

Chapter 11
Client retention

As with any businesses, client retention is crucial for success. A happy client will be one who then tells their friends and family how great you are as an aesthetic practitioner. However, the real secret to successful client retention should really be seen as client relationship management.

To benefit from this word-of-mouth, the treatments have to be the very best that they possibly can. It is also important to appreciate that how you handle clients is crucial because without good people skills and the talent to deliver top-quality treatments, your clinic will not be the success that you hope it will be.

Again, I was fortunate in teaming up with Dr Vincent Wong as a mentor because he is not only one of the best practitioners in the UK but also has extensive business experience now as well. I managed to benefit from that experience to create my successful business.

One of the issues about client retention is the problem that arises from the hard work a practitioner puts into attracting a client in the first place and then having to carry out a quality treatment. However, that work will then last between three and six months and the client may not want another treatment or, sadly, they may decide to find someone else to do it at a lower price.

As with many businesses one of the secrets to success is customer service, and that is also true for aesthetics. By being friendly and outgoing a client will appreciate being the focus of the practitioner's attention and will remember the level of service and quality they have received.

Indeed, some treatments will last for up to two years and it may simply be a case that the client can no longer remember who their practitioner was and the practice itself may have moved location. For many reasons, it is important to keep track of clients and it will become apparent that they may have gone somewhere else after a year and this will create a noticeable effect on the business.

There is a flipside to this and that is the clients are not only recommending you and your services but also remember you and will move heaven and earth to attend the practice for another treatment. This was apparent to me when one of my first clients flew in from Ghana a year after I carried out a treatment just for my help. I was really touched and the lady concerned ended-up staying for a week because she wanted a second treatment, a skin peel, and then left as a very happy client.

She is a lovely lady who is rather famous in her home country and I met her by chance when she came to visit me in my Harley Street clinic. I was so impressed that she flew in for me to treat her which underlines my belief that customer service is crucial for business success as an aesthetic practitioner.

However, I should also highlight that my client consultations are not like the mainstream approach. There isn't, for instance, a desk between me and the client where we have a formal conversation, and I then hand them a form to sign and take their money and do the treatment. I much prefer to learn more about them on a personal level and to make a strong connection so I understand their needs and wants more clearly and help meet them. I always try to form a good relationship and in the case of the lady from Ghana she ended up singing for me during the consultation!

Not all clients are going to be the friendliest or supportive. Some will have complaints, some will be unsatisfied but that is not usually down to the treatment offered, it is just that some clients like to complain without real grounds for doing so. It is also the reason why all aesthetic practitioners should not skimp on their indemnity insurance.

Essentially, the question of client retention fits with the previous chapter on how to promote yourself and the practice. On the one hand you have to promote the practice so people get to know of it and what treatments you are offering, and on the other hand you also need to deliver a high level of client satisfaction so that you will retain the client's loyalty which makes all of the effort worthwhile in attracting them in the first place.

I mentioned earlier about client relationship management and why it is important for a practice's future success. It is crucial that by defining which treatments you will offer, you will then create a quality base of clients. Establishing the client relationship helps with future success and it becomes easier to upsell other treatments when a client has come to trust you and enjoy the results of the treatment they received.

One of the handicaps that some people working in medicine, including pharmacists, have is that they sometimes do not have to concern themselves with recruiting clients since their business usually walks in through the door. This means those working in medicine may have limited experience of marketing, PR or how to develop their consultation skills to sell a product.

The other issue that is often overlooked by practitioners setting out with a new aesthetics practice is that their clinic must be comfortable and welcoming and that any staff working for you, even if you have established your clinic within a business, must also be professional and polite. This is not always the case with a medical practice because this level of customer service is not always as necessary because the patient will attend the clinic or surgery and will take time off work to do so. This means they are more forgiving than they would be for a private practice.

Some people will mistake the term 'client relationship management' as simply being something that they have to do with a client in a face-to-face situation such as a consultation. However, a true client relationship is much deeper and more involved and begins from the moment they make contact with your clinic. So, the relationship itself also includes offering after-hour appointments, making follow-up calls to ensure they are happy with their treatment and arranging their next appointment, offering flexible appointments and weekend services too. Essentially, it means that the practitioner must make a real and sustained effort in keeping their client happy and satisfied. By doing so the client will remain loyal to the practice and be willing to recommend your services.

There are various client relationship management software programs available and as your practice becomes more popular this may be a viable investment. The software will help you keep track of your client treatments, when they were contacted and when their next appointment is scheduled to be. The software also enables you to add notes such as recording when their birthdays are, the names of their children and so on so you can establish a personal dialogue when they turn up for a treatment or consultation. For the most part, practitioners should be organised enough not to have the software programs but this helps to underline just how important and complicated this subject can be.

Also, never lose sight of the fact that client relationship management is geared towards client retention because a client that regularly returns for treatment is spending money on a regular basis and does not have to be recruited to do so. There is no doubt that many new practices deal with new clients mainly and do not pay much attention to client retention. However, this means they are putting a lot of time, money and effort into client recruitment when they could make their work life so much easier and boost profitability at the same time. Some specialist relationship management software also keeps track of a client's spending habits and the demographic of your client base which will help a practitioner plan their marketing strategy and help put their financial forecast together. Some of this data will be invaluable to a business's success. If you opt not to use software to track a client, then you do need to be well organised and remember to communicate with emails and/or letters.

Alongside this direct client relationship management there are other issues that need to be addressed too. How a client is handled from the moment they call is important so you need to ensure that the receptionist is trained to deal with the call appropriately. The receptionist is the first contact the client will have with the business and they need to get this right from the very beginning; they need to deal with any enquiries, arrange appointments effectively and these calls need to be answered promptly. If you are working on your own, for instance after setting up your practice at home, it may be a worthwhile investment to outsource your telephone service so that the calls are answered independently of you and the client is dealt with professionally. While the outsourced service may not be able to access your appointments diary, they can arrange for you to call the client back at a convenient time.

Client retention works closely with client relationship management so that a practitioner will, on a regular basis, find out what their clients think about the service and the treatment they have received. Client feedback is the best way to record client satisfaction and if there are any issues then they need to be addressed quickly and effectively. For this reason, follow-up calls after a treatment will be important to see how the client feels and how they are recuperating. More importantly, it makes the client feel as though their practitioner does care about them and is taking time to find out.

We should also discuss the tricky subject of handling complaints from clients. When you are starting out, it may be good practice to establish an operations manual so that complaints are dealt with promptly and effectively. Indeed, dealing with complaints can prove to be an uncomfortable and unpleasant experience, however ignoring this will only result in further deterioration of the practitioner-client relationship. This may also be unavoidable as they may come about during a follow-up call and the issue will need to be addressed. Furthermore, a client may make a formal complaint and you to deal with this professionally too. Ensure that you spend time speaking with the client and listening to them and ensure you are delivering the treatment that is discussed and agreed upon. Many aesthetic practitioners will take photographs before and after a treatment which will help in dealing with a subsequent client complaint.

I would recommend that a practitioner who receives a complaint does not view it in negative terms; on the contrary this is an opportunity for a client to communicate with the practitioner. They may be complaining about the treatment or about the service they received, either way it is a legitimate complaint and not a direct criticism of the practitioner. Let us also not lose sight of the fact that the client could simply be disappointed with their treatment and move onto another practitioner rather than taking time and the effort in making a complaint. However, if the complaint is genuine then it is something to act upon and ensure it is not repeated so that your customer service levels remain high and clients have no grounds for complaint.

Another aspect of the client relationship is to analyse which treatments clients are coming in for. For instance, you may have regular clients over a long term, who have the same treatment every time and are not interested in other treatments being offered. There are other clients who will appear less frequently but who spend more; both of these are worthwhile opportunities for client retention. By developing a strategy that will develop the opportunities of your existing client base means that you do not have to spend as much time and effort in attracting new clients to boost turnover.

Everyone with an aesthetics practice should aim at over-delivery when it comes to customer service. It may also be a good idea to send a client an evaluation form so they can comment upon anything they liked or disliked. Again, this is an opportunity to put right even the smallest criticism to ensure that you deliver the very best in customer service. The form that is used could also be used as the basis for an ongoing client survey so you could ask questions about satisfaction with their waiting time, after-hours service and the treatment that they received. You could even ask about the billing process, how their appointment was managed and how professional and welcoming the staff were.

The bottom line when it comes to client relationship management is to deliver what your clients want and not what you think they want.

Conclusion

Hopefully, everyone reading 'A *Simple Guide To The World Of Aesthetics For Pharmacists'* will now be inspired and prepared to make their business venture the success it deserves to be. As a pharmacist, I can confirm that the skills we have and our experience lend themselves to success in this field. I have never looked back since making the switch and I hope that you do not either.

My main hope is that the book has explained in detail the simple steps necessary for setting up in practice and that the most important thing to consider is the strategic planning necessary to create a business plan and a financial forecast. The next most important steps are to consider carefully the client relationship necessary for building long-term profitability and that the client relationship marketing is not purely about promotion and advertising but also about the high level of customer service necessary and the soft skills you will need to promote yourself and your products.

I also appreciate that there is a big leap for many people who are leaving a medical background and moving into self-employment but the leap is not that large and the skills that you need are easily taught and there are others willing to help. I cannot stress enough how important it was for me to find a mentor who was not only experienced within aesthetics but who was willing to share their expertise with an enthusiastic newcomer. My mentor is Dr Vincent Wong and I will be eternally grateful for the time he has shown me to help me achieve the success I have within the industry.

If you do not like the sound of finding and then working alongside a mentor, I can heartily recommend contacting any of the many business organisations dedicated to helping start-ups and they offer their advice and experience willingly and for free.

Essentially, the last thought I want to leave readers with, is that setting up an aesthetics practise is straightforward. BUT the whole idea that I have put forward in this book is that the practice itself is structured in a way that uses innovative means to find new clients and then strives to over-deliver on its customer service to retain its clients and have a solid foundation for building future success. With a successful practice comes profitability and with profitability comes a high level of living standards that you have worked for and you should enjoy. For those who are skilled at developing their relationships with clients; the business will be the success you hope it will be.

I am genuinely interested in those who use this book as a template for setting-up their aesthetics practice and I wish you every success in your venture – let me know how you succeed and what you learn - which may be of use to others who want to follow in your footsteps.

Amar Suchde

About Amar Suchde (MPharm)

Amar Suchde is a fully qualified independent prescribing aesthetics pharmacist, specialising in non-surgical cosmetic treatments. He holds a Master's degree in Pharmacy from The University of Hertfordshire, one of the top pharmacy schools in the UK.

Prior to completing his training in medical aesthetics, Mr Suchde held various positions in community pharmacy where he gained experience in injectables, dermatology and general care of the health and well-being of his patients.

It was in 2014, where he was fortunate to have met Dr Vincent Wong, a world renowned doctor to the celebrities, who later went onto mentoring and training Mr Suchde.

A pioneer in his field, Mr Suchde went on to set up his own clinic, AMS Aesthetics, in London's prestigious Harley Street. It was from here that he set up another five venues in and around London, where he now has a loyal and dedicated following of clients from London, America, Australia, Africa and many other countries from around the world.

Committed to the highest standards of aesthetic treatments, Mr Suchde mentors junior pharmacists and has created a platform, with Dr Wong, for pharmacists to embark on a similar journey as him and provides regular one-to-one mentoring and training courses to help one achieve a Level 7 postgraduate qualification in cosmetic injectables, all in line with the new HEE guidelines whereby pharmacists and other practitioners who want to carry out non-surgical cosmetic treatments must complete a postgraduate level qualification to progress in the industry.

In need of Mr Suchde's expert opinion, he has featured in a Safety in Beauty documentary called "Life is Beauty-full" on SKY TV and written articles in the popular press. He has also appeared on radio chat shows and has carried out various medical clinical studies with leading doctors from the world of aesthetics.

If you are interested in Mr Suchde's elite mentorship package, where you will follow his exact steps and be mentored by him and various leading doctors in the industry, including the famous Dr V Wong, then please do not hesitate to get in contact at Amar@pharm-aesthetics.uk.

Having such a friendly and welcoming nature, Mr Suchde will enjoy hearing from you and will help you to become the best you.

Made in the USA
Middletown, DE
07 September 2020